Learning About Cells

By

DEBBIE ROUTH

COPYRIGHT © 2006 Mark Twain Media, Inc.

ISBN-13: 978-1-58037-321-0
ISBN-10: 1-58037-321-6

Printing No. CD-404050

Mark Twain Media, Inc., Publishers
Distributed by Carson-Dellosa Publishing Company, Inc.

Table of Contents

Introduction

Welcome to the fascinating world of cells. In this book, you will learn many things about the biology of the cells in your body. If you think about it, you are nothing more than the sum of your cells. You could compare your body to a brick building—the building is the sum of all of its bricks. Each brick is the basic unit of structure of the building. The basic unit of structure in everything living is the **cell**. The cells in your body perform certain tasks, as you will soon discover.

This book will help you understand the amazing concepts of **cytology**—the study of cells. You will learn what a cell is, who discovered cells, how the cell theory was developed, the difference between a unicellular and a multicellular organism (living thing), how cells are organized, the parts and functions of the cell, and how and why it is important to study cells. It is important that you remember that the simplest unit of life, the cell, is very complex and an integrated piece of the machinery that makes up all living things and how they work.

As student observers, you will use many scientific process skills to discover the world of cells. The reinforcement worksheets that follow each lesson will serve as follow-up activities for checking understanding. They often contain one higher-level thinking question to stretch your mind.

How about it, student observers, are you ready to put on those thinking caps and use your process skills to observe, analyze, debate, design, and report? This unit contains a variety of lessons that will help you practice scientific processes, as you make new discoveries about cells and gain a better understanding of the microbe world.

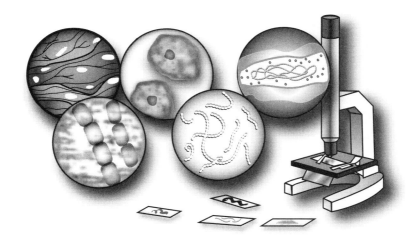

Teacher note: This book supports the National Science Education Standards and is designed to supplement your existing science curriculum. Each lesson opens with a manageable amount of text for the student to read. The succeeding pages contain exercises and illustrations that are varied and plentiful. Phonetic spellings and simple definitions for terms are also included to assist the student. The lessons may be used as a complete unit for the entire class or as supplemental material for the reluctant learner. The tone of the book is informal; a dialogue is established between the book and the student.

What Are Cells?

A **cell** is often defined as the basic unit of structure in all living things. In other words, all living things are made up of cells. They are the smallest things that can be called "alive." Most living things are made up of many cells (**multicellular**) that collectively make up the **organism** (living thing). A brick building is made up of many bricks, which are its basic units of structure. Cells are like the bricks of a building—they are the building blocks of life. All living things are made up of one or many cells. Depending on their size and complexity, many living things are made up of billions, or even trillions of cells. Cells make up who you are and how you work. Cells make up your blood, bone, skin, nerves, and muscles. Cells carry out all your life processes—they are wonderfully specialized to do certain jobs in different regions of your body. Did you know that there are approximately 200 different types of cells in your body? As an example, do you know what cells cover and protect your body? If you answered skin cells, you are absolutely correct.

Listed below are some of the jobs of the specialized cells in your body:
- Movement of body parts: muscle cells
- Support and protection of body: bone cells
- Sending and receiving of messages: nerve cells
- Fighting disease: immune cells
- Transporting materials to all your parts: blood cells

Some living things are made up of only one cell (**unicellular**) and carry out all the basic life activities within that single cell. The simplest cells in existence are those of **bacteria**, which are little containers of DNA. They are so simple they do not even have a true nucleus. You will learn more about bacterium cells in another lesson. The fact that they are so simple does not mean that they are unsuccessful, as they are found everywhere and in enormous numbers.

Living Kingdoms

At one time, all organisms were thought to be plants or animals. The development of the microscope led scientists to the discovery of new living things called **microscopic organisms**. These newly discovered organisms were too small to be seen with the unaided eye. These microscopic organisms (**microbes**) were placed into another kingdom. As microscopes improved, scientists learned that all microbes were not the same. Some microbes didn't have a nucleus or other cell structures, so they were placed into a group of their own. Then scientists looked closer at the cells of fungi and learned that they were not like plants and needed a group all their own. Living things share certain characteristics; for example, all living things carry out basic life activities. However, all living things can be very different. Scientists have divided the world of living things into one of these five main groups, called **kingdoms**.

What Are Cells? (cont.)

1. **Monera** (muh NER uh) – Monera means "alone." This kingdom has only one kind of or-ganism—bacteria. Bacterium cells are one-celled (unicellular) organisms without a true nucleus; some are able to move about.

2. **Protista** (PRŌH tis tuh) – Protists are mostly one-celled organisms that do have a true nucleus. Some are protozoas (animal-like) and move to obtain food. Others are algae (plant-like) and can make their own food. Some protists are fungus-like and obtain their food from what they grow on.

3. **Fungi** (FUN jī) – are mostly many-celled (multicellular) organisms that have cells with nuclei and cell walls but lack chlorophyll, so they cannot make their own food. They cannot move about. Instead, they absorb their food from whatever they are growing on.

4. **Plants** – are many-celled organisms that have cells with true nuclei, cell walls, and chlo-rophyll. They cannot move about; they use sunlight to make their own food.

5. **Animals** – are many-celled organisms that have cells with true nuclei but lack cell walls and chlorophyll. They move about in order to eat other organisms.

As new information becomes available, these kingdoms may change again. Some sci-entists want to add a sixth kingdom to include **viruses**. At this time, viruses are not considered "alive" and have not been placed into any of the kingdoms of living things.

Name: _____ Date: _____

What Are Cells?: *Reinforcement Activity*

To the student observer: Explain what a cell is. (Be specific in your answer.)

_____

_____

_____

Analyze: What is the relationship between the improved microscopes and the discoveries made about cells?

_____

_____

Part I. Directions: Complete the following sentences.

1. _____ are the building blocks of life.

2. The cells in your body are _____ to do specific jobs.

3. Cells can be _____ in all parts of your body.

4. Multicellular organisms have _____ cells.

5. Unicellular organisms have only _____ cell.

6. Bacteria are the _____ cells.

Part II. Directions: Match the specialized cells below to their specific job.

_____ 1. Muscle cells   A. Cover and protect the body

_____ 2. Bone cells   B. Transport materials to all parts of your body

_____ 3. Nerve cells   C. Help the parts of your body move

_____ 4. Immune cells   D. Support and protect your body

_____ 5. Blood cells   E. Help your body fight disease and infection

_____ 6. Skin cells   F. Receive and send messages within your body

Part III. Directions: List the five kingdoms (main groups) of living things.

a. _____   b. _____   c. _____

d. _____   e. _____

Let's Get Organized!

Cell Organization

You have learned that all living things are made up of one or more cells. This includes plants, animals, and many microbes. **Microbes**, unicellular organisms made up of only one cell, cause many infectious diseases. **Histologists**, scientists who study cells, have learned many new things. They have noticed that cells have tiny structures inside of them. From studying different cells in different organisms, they discovered that many of these structures are typically found in all cells.

Organelles

Scientists named the tiny organs inside the cell **organelles**. Each organelle performs specific functions for the cell. The cell works in much the same way as a busy manufacturing plant. Anything that works, works best if someone is in control. Most things that work need energy to keep things humming along. A cell, like a manufacturer, transforms simple materials into complex substances and packages them to be delivered where they are needed. These are just a few of the responsibilities of various cell organelles. Organelles are the many tiny parts within a cell that make the cell run smoothly and keep it alive.

Cells

In multicellular organisms, histologists learned that certain cells that did the same job were similar in their size and shape. As an example, nerve cells are like telephone wires inside your body. They carry messages to all parts of the body by an impulse. They are all long and thin and do the same job. Nerve cells make up nerve tissue. A group of cells that are similar and act together to do a certain job make up a larger part of your body called **tissue**.

Tissue

A **tissue** is a group of similar cells that work together to do the same job. Each cell in a tissue does its part to keep the tissue alive. For example, muscle cells are joined together to make muscle tissue. These tissues include leg muscles, arm muscles, and your heart muscle. Cells in your muscle tissue work together to make your body move. You have four main kinds of tissue: muscle tissue, covering tissue, connective tissue, and nerve tissue. Tissues in your body that are similar and do the same job are organized into a somewhat larger part of your body called **organs**.

Organs

An **organ** is a structure that is made up of two or more different types of tissue that work together to do the same job. An organ is the main working part of plants and animals. Each organ does a specific job to make all your systems run smoothly. Your heart is an organ made up of muscle tissue, nerve tissue, and blood tissue. The heart is made up of muscle tissue that contracts, making the heart pump blood. The nerve tissue receives messages from your body that tells the heart how fast to beat or pump the blood. Your body has many organs: stomach, kidneys, and brain to name a few. A group of organs working together to perform a certain job make up an **organ system**.

Let's Get Organized! (cont.)

Organ Systems

A group of similar organs doing the same job make up an **organ system**. Your heart, arteries, veins, and capillaries make up your circulatory system. In many-celled organisms, several systems work together in order to perform life functions efficiently. You have various systems that work together to keep you alive. Organelles make up your cells, your cells make up your tissues, your tissues make up your organs, and your organs make up the systems that keep you alive. You have seven main systems: skeletal, muscular, digestive, circulatory, respiratory, excretory, and nervous.

EXAMPLES OF THE WAY CELLS ARE ORGANIZED IN THE BODY

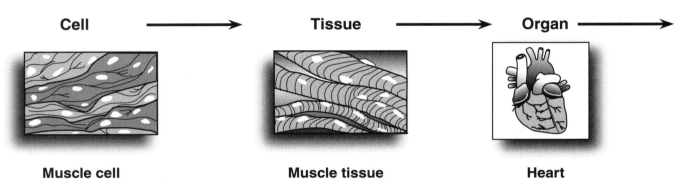

Cell → **Tissue** → **Organ** →

Muscle cell   Muscle tissue   Heart

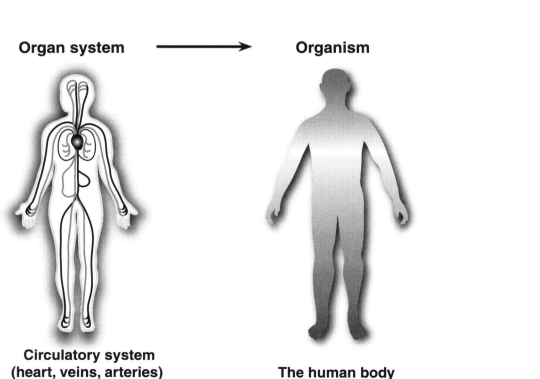

Organ system → **Organism**

**Circulatory system
(heart, veins, arteries)**   **The human body**

Name: _____ Date: _____

Let's Get Organized!: *Reinforcement Activity*

To the student observer: Cut out the terms and arrows on the next page and arrange the terms with an arrow between them so they make the most sense. *Hint:* Since there are only five arrows, you will only use six terms. One term will be left out.

Directions: When you have a satisfactory arrangement, write the words and draw the arrows in the correct arrangement in the spaces provided.

_____   _____   _____

_____   _____   _____

Analyze: Which term did you leave out? How did you arrange the terms and why?

_____

_____

Directions: Complete the following sentences.

1. _____ are the tiny parts inside a cell.

2. _____ that do the same job are similar in size and shape.

3. Similar cells that work together make up _____.

4. A(n) _____ is a structure made up of two or more different types of tissue.

5. A group of similar organs doing the same job make up a(n) _____.

6. List the seven main systems that work together to make up a human being.

   a. _____   e. _____

   b. _____   f. _____

   c. _____   g. _____

   d. _____

7. List the four main types of tissue found in your body:

   a. _____   b. _____

   c. _____   d. _____

Name: _____ Date: _____

Let's Get Organized!: *Cell Organization Cards*

MOLECULES	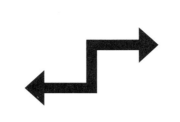	SYSTEMS
ORGANELLES		TISSUES
	CELLS	
ORGANS		ORGANISMS

The History of Cells

Pioneers in Cells

We now know the basic unit of all living things is the cell, just as the atom is the basic unit of matter. It was the work and dedication of several scientists that has led us to the place we are today. Some say our time may be looked back upon as the golden age of biology. The reason for this is the fact that the molecules of life can now be analyzed by new techniques to determine their roles and structures in the cell. We have learned many things that have enhanced our understanding of the cause of disease. The effects of this ongoing explosion of knowledge still remain to be seen.

Discovery

The first person to see **cells**, the building blocks of life, was an English scientist, Robert Hooke. In 1665, he used one of the earliest microscopes to view thin slices of cork. Cork is found in some plants. The first cells observed were no longer living. Hooke found that cork was composed of a honeycomb of hollow chambers that he called cells. What he saw in the microscope was actually the spaces in the cork where cells once lived. Hooke decided to call the hollow structures *cells* because they reminded him of the small rooms in which monks slept.

Anton van Leeuwenhoek (AN tun van LAY vun hook) was one of the earliest and most successful observers of cells. He was the first person to observe living cells. He observed single-celled organisms swimming about in a drop of pond water. He used a simple microscope that he had made, using a tiny bead for a lens. He manufactured over two hundred simple microscopes that allowed him to observe the wonderful world of tiny "animalcules." These microbes are now known as **bacteria** and **protozoans**.

The Cell Theory

By the 1800s, better microscopes were being made, and scientists had many ideas about cells. Their ideas were put together into a theory, an idea that is consistently supported by data. The credit for the theory goes to two German scientists, Matthias Schleiden, a **botanist** (one who studies plants), and Theodor Schwann, a **zoologist** (one who studies animals). Schleiden discovered that plants were made up of cells, and Schwann reported the same to be true of animals; this discovery led to the first part of the Cell Theory. Together they hypothesized that all living things are made up of cells; this was the second part of the Cell Theory. Several years later, Randolph Virchow, a German doctor, hypothesized that cells didn't just form on their own. He believed that cells divide from existing cells to form new cells. This led to the third part of the Cell Theory. The **Cell Theory** is one of the major theories in science. It is not based on the hypotheses and observations of only one scientist but is the result of the discoveries of many scientists. Today, the Cell Theory serves as the basis upon which **histologists** (scientists who study cells) have built their ongoing explosion of knowledge and information in cell biology.

The **Cell Theory** states that:

- All organisms are made up of one or more cells.
- Cells are the basic units of structure and function in all organisms.
- All cells come from other cells that already exist.

Name: _____ Date: _____

The History of Cells: *Reinforcement Activity*

To the student observer: List the pioneers in the study of cells.

_____

_____

_____

Analyze: Do you believe the cork that Hooke observed could produce new cells? Explain.

_____

_____

_____

Directions: Complete the following sentences.

1. _____ are the building blocks of life.

2. _____ was the first person to see cells.

3. The first cells observed were dead cells in thin slices of _____.

4. _____ was the first person to observe living cells in a drop of pond water.

5. The _____ _____ is one of the major theories in science.

6. The work of _____, _____, and _____ led to the development of the Cell Theory.

7. _____ are scientists who study cells.

8. List the three parts of the Cell Theory.

   a. _____

   b. _____

   c. _____

What Is a Microscope?

Studying Cells

You have learned that cells come in different sizes. Most cells are so small that they are invisible to the unaided eye. They can only be seen with the use of an important scientific tool called the **microscope**. A microscope is an instrument that magnifies very tiny things in order to make them appear larger. Before we can observe and study cells, we must first learn to use the microscope. *Micro* means "very small," while *scope* means "to look at." Some microscopes are very simple and are similar to a hand lens or magnifying glass. Have you used a hand lens before? If you were to look at a spider with a hand lens, you would be able to see tiny structures on the spider that you couldn't see without the hand lens.

Most microscopes and magnifying glasses use light and lenses (curved pieces of glass) to magnify the object. The lens bends the light rays in order to make an enlarged image. A lens maker, Anton van Leeuwenhoek, invented the first simple microscope. Later, two Dutch eyeglass makers, Hans and Zacharias Janssen, invented the first compound microscope (a microscope that uses more than one lens). Their microscopes had a lens at each end of a tube, but the lenses were of poor quality, and the images were blurred and distorted.

It wasn't until 1670, that the quality of the lenses improved enough to produce a clear image in the field of view. A **field of view** is the circular image you see when you look through the eyepiece. When a cell is viewed under a light microscope, some of the tiny structures inside the cell can be seen. These tiny structures are called **organelles**. You will learn about cell organelles in another lesson. Microscopes can magnify an object only so much before the image of the object becomes blurry.

Lenses

As you probably know, a **lens** is a curved piece of glass. Some lenses have one curved surface and one flat surface, while others have two curved surfaces. Lenses that curve outward like the surface of a sphere are **convex** lenses. Lenses that curve inward like the inside of a hollow ball are **concave** lenses. Some lenses are a combination of both.

DIFFERENT TYPES OF LENSES

| Concave | Concave on both sides | Convex on both sides | Convex | Convex and Concave |

What Is a Microscope? (cont.)

Kinds of Microscopes

There are many different kinds of microscopes. Microscopes are either **simple** (containing one lens) or **compound** (containing two or more lenses). A simple microscope is like a magnifying glass. Have you ever used a hand lens before? If so, you have used a simple microscope.

Light microscopes use light and lenses to magnify (enlarge) things. The microscopes you use in your classroom are compound light microscopes. They let light pass through the object and then through two or more lenses. Convex lenses are used as magnifying lenses and bend the light toward your eye. They usually have an eyepiece lens with the power to magnify something ten times. The objective lenses vary in power.

Using the different objective lenses changes the magnification of the microscope. The **low-power** objective is usually a 10X magnification lens. It shows more of the object but less detail. The **high-power objective** contains the lens with the greatest amount of magnification. It shows less of the object you are viewing but shows it in greater detail. The magnification power of a microscope is the product of the magnifying power of the lenses. Take the magnification of the eyepiece and multiply it by the magnification of the objective (nosepiece) lens to determine the total magnification of the microscope. A standard microscope can make objects appear 50 to 500 times larger than their actual size.

Calculating the Magnification of a Microscope
Eyepiece Lens X Objective Lens = Total Magnification

Eyepiece lens =   10X (magnification)
Objective lens =   40X (magnification)
Total magnification =   400X (the product of 10 x 40)

Electron microscopes use electrons to magnify objects; this type of microscope does not use light. Electrons are the particles that light up your television screen. When a cell is viewed under an electron microscope, its organelles can be seen clearly. The **transmission electron microscope (TEM)** is used to study parts inside a living cell. The **scanning electron microscope (SEM)** is used to view dead cells and tissue. It is also used to see the surfaces of the whole object. These microscopes are very expensive and are not likely to be found in your classroom. They are used in research centers, hospitals, and doctors' offices. Electron microscopes can magnify objects 300,000 times their actual size.

Your classroom may have a **light stereoscope microscope**; this type of microscope is used to see three-dimensional views of objects too thick to let light pass through. For example, if you wanted to see an earthworm up close, you would use one of these microscopes. This microscope has two ocular (eyepiece) lenses.

What Is a Microscope? (cont.)

DIFFERENT TYPES OF MICROSCOPES

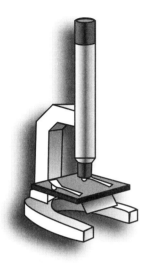

Simple Microscope

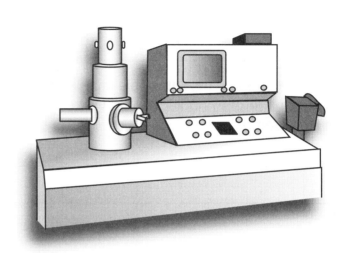

Scanning Electron Microscope (SEM)

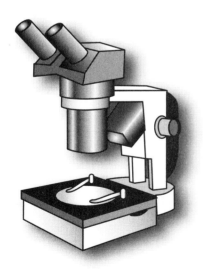

Light Stereoscope Microscope

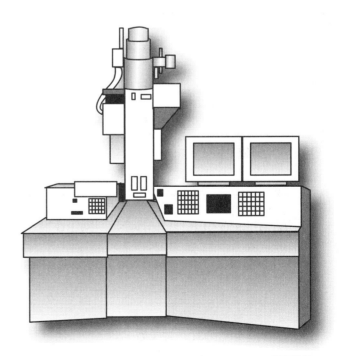

Transmission Electron Microscope (TEM)

Name: _____ Date: _____

What Is a Microscope?: *Reinforcement Activity*

To the student observer: What does the word *microscope* mean?

_____

_____

_____

Analyze: When you change the objective lens from low to high power, what effect does that have on the image of the object being viewed? (How does it appear to change what you see in the microscope?)

_____

_____

_____

Directions: Answer the following questions.

1. How does a compound microscope differ from a simple microscope?

    _____

    _____

2. If the eyepiece of the microscope has a 10X lens and you are using a 55X high-power

    objective lens, what is the total magnification in high power? _____

3. What kind of microscope is found in most classrooms?

    _____

4. What kind of lens curves outward like a sphere? _____

5. What kind of microscope has the greatest magnification? (used to study cell structures)

    _____

6. Which microscope would you use if the object is too thick to let light pass through it?

    _____

How to Use a Microscope

A License to Learn

Observers, are you ready to get your license to use a microscope and learn about cells? Microscopes are fun and easy to use if you know their parts and what they do. Microscopes are very expensive and require knowledge to use them properly. Always use both hands to carry a microscope. One hand should be on the arm, and the other hand should be under the base. Always store microscopes with the low-power objective in place. When focusing your microscope, use the low-power objective first. All microscopes have the same basic parts. Read about the parts of the microscope and locate each part in the drawing below. The sheet on the next page will help you study for your microscope test. Once you've passed your test, you will get a license to operate a microscope and study cells.

Arm: supports the body tube and is used to carry the microscope.

Base: supports the microscope and is used to carry it; the bottom part of the microscope.

Body tube: Light passes through this hollow tube; it also maintains the correct distance between the eyepiece lens and the objective lens.

Coarse adjustment knob: turns to raise and lower the body tube or stage for focusing; always use this knob first.

Diaphragm (DY uh fram)**:** changes the amount of light that enters the body tube

Eyepiece: contains the lens you look through; the top part of the microscope.

Fine adjustment knob: moves slightly and is used to sharpen the image.

Mirror or light source: is used to send light up through the hole in the stage, object, and lenses.

Nosepiece: holds the objective lenses and rotates to change the magnification.

Objective lenses: usually range from 10X to 40X magnification; located on the nosepiece.

Stage: supports the object (microscope slide) being viewed.

Stage clips: hold the microscope slide in place.

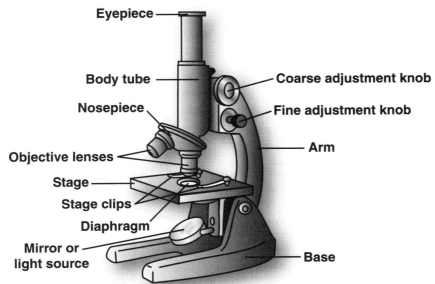

Name: _____ Date: _____

The Parts of a Microscope

Directions: Use this sheet to label the parts of the microscope. On your own paper, explain the function of each part. This will make a great study tool to gain your license to use a microscope. Good luck, observers!

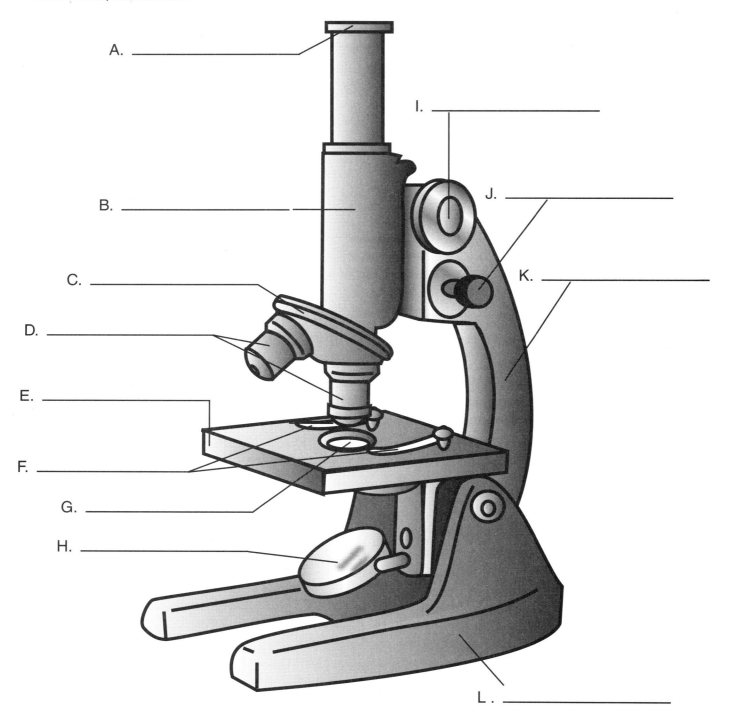

A. _____

B. _____

C. _____

D. _____

E. _____

F. _____

G. _____

H. _____

I. _____

J. _____

K. _____

L. _____

Name: _____ Date: _____

Microscope Quiz

To the student observer: After passing this quiz, you will have successfully demonstrated your knowledge of microscope parts and handling rules to gain your microscope license.

Directions: Match the microscope parts listed with the proper function.

Microscope Parts

A. Eyepiece   B. Low-power objective   C. Coarse adjustment knob
D. Diaphragm   E. High-power objective   F. Mirror   G. Arm
H. Fine adjustment knob   I. Base   J. Stage clips
K. Revolving nosepiece   L. Stage   M. Body tube

Functions

_____ 1. Moves body tube or stage up and down for focusing

_____ 2. Supports the microscope slide and viewing object

_____ 3. Supports the body tube and is used to carry the microscope

_____ 4. Contains the lens you look through

_____ 5. Reflects light up through the diaphragm, stage, viewing object, and lenses

_____ 6. Provides the least magnification; usually 10X

_____ 7. Supports the microscope

_____ 8. Hold the microscope slide in place

_____ 9. Provides the greatest magnification; usually 40X

_____ 10. Controls the amount of light that enters the body tube

_____ 11. Passageway for light and maintains the correct distance between the lenses

_____ 12. Moves slightly and is used to sharpen the image of the object you are viewing

_____ 13. Holds high- and low-power objectives; rotates to change magnification

Microscope License

Congratulations! You have demonstrated the knowledge of microscope parts and handling rules required to operate a light microscope and are hereby awarded this license.

Student Name: _____

Authorized by: _____

Valid: For Life

Do You Know Your Cells?

Main Types of Cells

There are basically two main types of cells: **eukaryotes** (YEW kar ee oats) and **prokaryotes** (PRO kar ee oats). Cells with a true membrane-bound nucleus are called eukaryotic cells. Most cells, including all plants and animals, are eukaryotic, which means that they have all of their nuclear material inside a true **nucleus,** or the control center of the cell. Prokaryotic cells do not have a membrane-bound nucleus. They have nuclear material floating around "freely" inside the gel-like cytoplasm but do not have a true nucleus. The simplest cells in existence, bacteria and their relatives, are the only members of this type of cell. Prokaryotic bacteria are little more than a membrane-enclosed container of DNA and other enzymes needed for metabolism and reproduction. The DNA is organized into a single loop (circle) that floats inside the cell.

Two Kinds of Cells

- **Eukaryotic:** a cell with nuclear material inside a true (membrane-bound) nucleus.
- **Prokaryotic:** a cell with nuclear material floating "freely" inside the cytoplasm; it has no true membrane-bound nucleus.

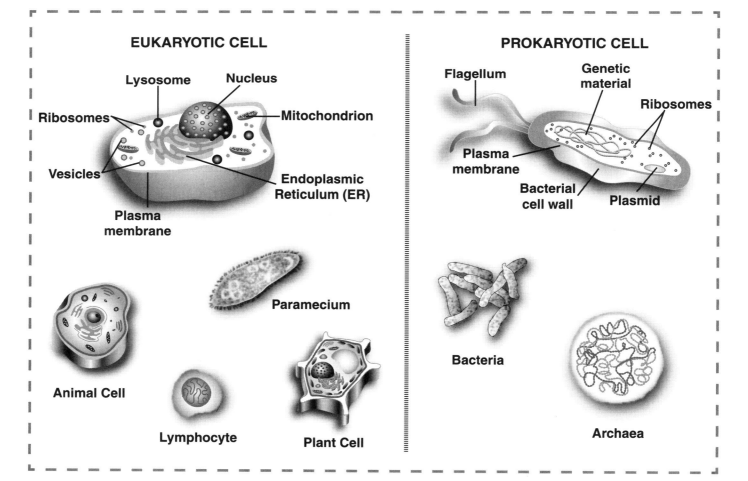

The Main Parts of a Cell

What Are the Main Parts of a Cell?

Most cells have several factors in common. In this lesson, you will learn to be able to identify the three main parts found in most cells and describe their functions. The three main parts of most cells and their descriptions are shown below. Most cells include a nucleus, the cytoplasm, and the cell membrane.

Nucleus

Long strands of chromosomes that contain **deoxyribonucleic acid (DNA)** are located in the **nucleus**. DNA is the hereditary material or the genetic blueprint for the organism. This is important for the reproduction of new cells. The nucleus is usually found near the cell's center and can be round or egg-shaped. It is usually darker in color than the rest of the cell. It is the control center of the cell. It controls all of the life processes that go on inside the cell. It is often referred to as the "brains" of the outfit.

Cytoplasm

Most of the cell is made up of **cytoplasm**. It contains all the living material in a cell except for the nucleus. This gel-like area of the cell contains the chemicals needed by the cell. It resembles the white part of a raw egg. This is where most of the activities take place, as it contains all of the other cell parts, or **organelles**.

Cell Membrane

The **cell membrane** is a thin layer that encloses the cell and controls the movement of materials into and out of the cell; it offers protection and shapes the cell. It surrounds and holds the cell together. It is often referred to as the "gatekeeper" for the cell. The cell membrane seems to know which materials to let into the cell and which materials to let out of the cell.

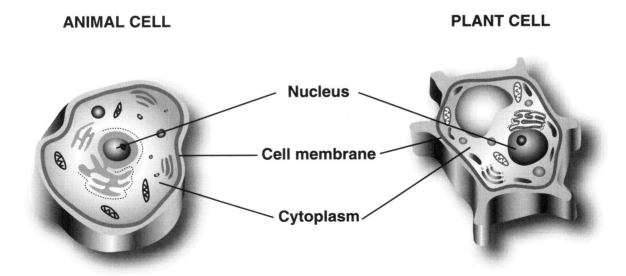

ANIMAL CELL   **PLANT CELL**

Nucleus

Cell membrane

Cytoplasm

What Are Other Cell Parts?

Organelles

You can compare the cell to a school. There are many components of the school that help it run. Each component has a special job to do, and they must all work together to run the school. The components of the cell are called **organelles** (or guh NELS). Organelles are small structures that float in the gel-like cytoplasm. Each organelle must perform its unique job to keep the cell working properly. The cell is a unique miniaturization of life's functions. It moves, reacts, protects itself, grows, and reproduces more cells like itself. It has a control center, power plants, internal communication, and construction and manufacturing elements. Now that you know the three main parts of a cell, let's take a closer look at the amazing components called organelles that are responsible for keeping the cell alive.

Business in a Small World

Keeping the cell in operation is the work of many different organelles. Of course, you've already learned that the nucleus is the part of the cell that keeps everything in control. Cells need power (energy) to keep things humming along. Where does the energy come from that keeps a runner going at full-blast? It comes from a tiny, sausage-shaped pod with the Greek name **mitochondrion** (MYT uh KAHN dree un). Its job is to produce the power or energy needed by burning food obtained or produced in the cell. The mitochondrion is the seat of power—the powerhouse of the cell.

The cell needs to be able to deliver the goods produced just like a manufacturing plant needs to deliver goods to its customers. The **endoplasmic reticulum** (EN doh PLAS mik ri TIK yoo lum), or ER, is a tube-like network that enables the cell to transport (deliver) material where it is needed. ER is the transfer-and-delivery setup. The prime building material for the cell is **protein**. All living things need protein for growth. Inside every cell are small round structures that make the protein, called **ribosomes**. Sometimes they operate in isolation, but usually they are found along the edge or linked to the ER. The protein is then wrapped or packaged for shipment in a complex called the **Golgi** (GOL jee) **body**. Golgi bodies, stacks of protein-filled sacs, store and package the protein the cell exports. As needed, bits of the Golgi complex breaks off, and the protein, neatly packaged, goes to market.

The **vacuoles** (VAK yoo wohls), another cell organelle, are liquid-filled spaces inside the cell that serve as storage bins. They store water, food, and waste for the cell. Inside plant cells, you will find that the vacuole is very large. Animal cells have numerous small vacuoles.

Other organelles in the cytoplasm of plant cells are green, disc-shaped structures that contain chlorophyll called **chloroplasts**. It is the chloroplast that allows the plant to make its own food.

A typical animal cell

A typical plant cell

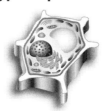

Comparing Plant and Animal Cells

All cells are classified into one of four categories. **Free-living plant cells** form single-celled, plant-like organisms. **Free-living animal cells** form single-celled, animal-like organisms. **Associated plant cells** live in communities in association with each other to form the multicellular organism that makes its own food—trees, bushes, and flowering plants make up this group. **Associated animal cells** also live in communities in association with each other to form the multicellular organism that moves about in order to obtain food—dogs, butterflies, elephants, and people make up this group.

Plant cells are different from animal cells. They have a rectangular shape and are more rigid because they have a non-living structure called a **cell wall** that surrounds the cell membrane. They also contain tiny disc-shaped structures called **chloroplasts**. Chloroplasts allow the cell to make its own food by a process called **photosynthesis**. After reading this lesson, you should be able to identify the ways in which plant and animal cells are alike and different.

As you have already learned, all living things are made up of cells. Some living things, such as plants and animals, are made up of many cells. These cells have many similarities as well as many differences.

Similarities: Cell Comparisons
- Both have a cell membrane that surrounds the cell.
- Both are filled with a gel-like substance called cytoplasm that contains all of the materials needed by the cell.
- Both have a nucleus where DNA is stored.
- Both have ribosomes that make proteins needed by the cell.
- Both have mitochondria, or a power source, that breaks down food and releases energy.
- Both have vacuoles that contain food, water, and waste products. Animal cells usually have more and smaller vacuoles than plant cells do.
- Both have endoplasmic reticulum, or ER, a system of tubes that transport proteins.
- Both have Golgi bodies, which package and distribute proteins outside the cell.

Differences: Cell Contrasts
- A plant cell has a cell wall that surrounds the cell membrane and provides shape and support; an animal cell does not.
- Plant cells have chloroplasts for photosynthesis; animal cells do not.
- Plant cells are more rectangular or brick-shaped; animal cells are more rounded.
- Plants use chloroplasts to store energy in sugar; animal cells use mitochondria to release energy stored in food.
- Plants have only one large vacuole; animal cells have several small ones.
- Plant cells lack lysosomes; animal cells have these.

Name: _____ Date: _____

The Parts of a Cell: *Reinforcement Activity*

To the student observer: Explain what organelles are.

_____

_____

Analyze: Which cells would contain more mitochondria: skin cells or muscle cells? Why?

_____

_____

_____

Directions: Answer the following questions.

1. Why does a cell need energy? _____

   _____

2. List the three main parts of the cell and describe the function of each.

   a. _____

   b. _____

   c. _____

3. Which structure in a cell makes protein? _____

4. Which structure is responsible for the transportation and delivery of materials?

   _____

5. What is stored in cell vacuoles? _____

6. What are three ways in which plant cells differ from animal cells?

   a. _____

   b. _____

   c. _____

Name: _____ Date: _____

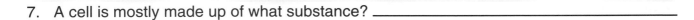

The Parts of a Cell: *Reinforcement Activity*

7. A cell is mostly made up of what substance? _____

8. Based on what you know about the cell membrane, what do you think the job of a nuclear membrane would be?

   _____

   _____

9. Modeling: Draw a typical animal cell in the box below and label the parts using the following terms: cell membrane, nucleus, cytoplasm, ER, ribosomes, vacuoles, mitochondria, and Golgi bodies.

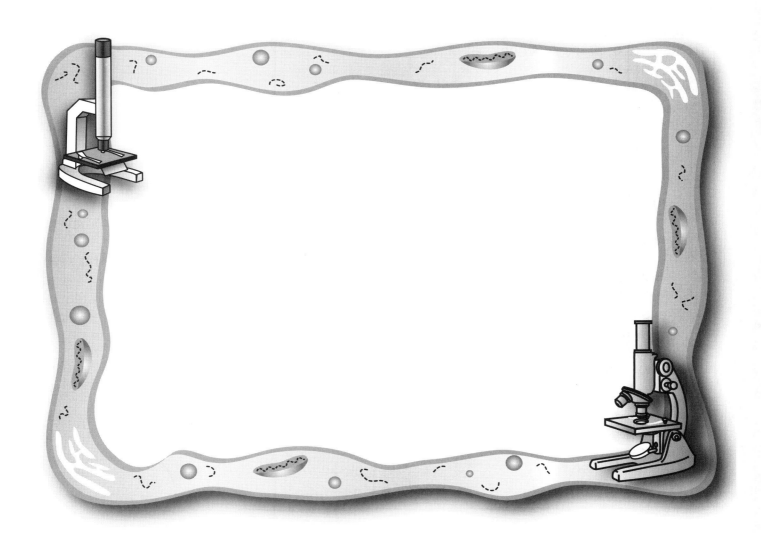

Name: _____ Date: _____

Living Things Are Made of These?

Viewing Cells Lab

That's right, you and every living thing around you is made up of these small units called cells. This lab will clear up any misconceptions you may have about this theory that all living things are made of cells. You will learn the correct way to prepare a microscope slide and practice preparing things for viewing under a microscope. You will see the tiny individual units (cells) of which each living thing is made. You will have the opportunity to compare plant and animal cells.

Materials:

Onion
Elodea leaf (an aquarium plant that is thin so light will pass through easily)
Slides and cover slips
Microscope
Needle
Two eyedroppers (one for water and one for staining solution)
Beaker or container of water
Iodine stain or staining solution in a small beaker or container
Toothpicks or prepared cheek cell slides

Procedure for viewing onion and elodea cells

Onion cells and elodea leaf cells:

1. Obtain a small piece of onion and elodea leaf from your teacher.
2. Place the elodea leaf on the microscope slide and add a drop of water. Place the cover on its edge and gently drop it down over the object so you push out any air bubbles in the water.
3. Use a needle to peel a thin, clear piece of tissue from the inside section of an onion. You may need to ask for assistance on this step.
4. Place the onion tissue on the slide. Try to place it smoothly on the slide and avoid having any wrinkles in the tissue.
5. Add a drop of staining solution or iodine to the thinly peeled slice of onion tissue. The stain helps to reveal the clear tissue's individual cells.
6. View the onion and elodea under the microscope. Use the low-power objective first to focus and view the plant cells. Then, taking care not to damage the lens or break the slide, view under high power.
7. Many small cells should be observed in your field of view.
8. Draw what you observed in your field of view below.

Onion Cells

Low Power   **High Power**

Elodea Leaf Cells

Low Power   **High Power**

Name: _____ Date: _____

  Living Things Are Made of These? (cont.)

Procedure for viewing cheek cells

Cheek cells:

1. Add a drop of staining solution to the center of a clean slide.
2. With the blunt end of a toothpick, gently scrape the inside lining of your cheek. Stir the end of the toothpick in the staining solution. (*Note:* you will not see anything in the solution.)
3. Place a cover slip over the drop of staining solution (using the proper technique). View under low power and then, with care, high power just as you did with the plant cells.
4. Many cells will be visible. They will be more rounded in appearance.
5. Cheek cells can be difficult to obtain, so your teacher may have already prepared slides for you to view. If you are using already prepared slides, skip the first two steps. Prepared slides save a great deal of time in this lab.
6. Draw what you observed in your field of view below.

Cheek Cells

Low Power   **High Power**

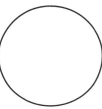   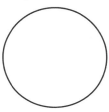

Label the cells below correctly.

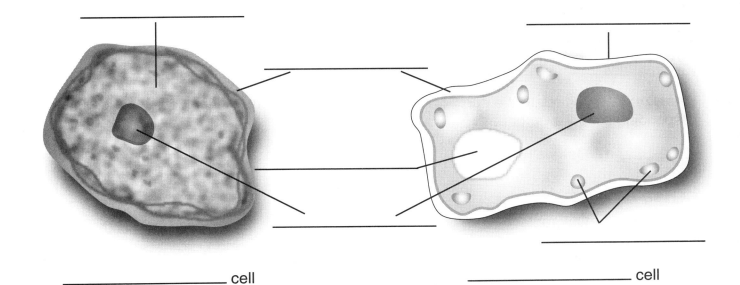

_____ cell   _____ cell

Name: _____ Date: _____

Living Things Are Made of These?: *Lab Report*

Problem: Are living things really made up of many small units called cells? Explain.

_____

_____

To the student observer: Mark each column below with a check mark for the cell or cells the words or phrases describe. The completed table will provide you with information to evaluate the differences between plant and animal cells. The first one has been done for you.

Description	Onion	Elodea	Cheek
1. rectangular or brick-like shape	✓	✓	
2. chloroplasts			
3. nucleus			
4. circular in shape			
5. cell wall			
6. cytoplasm			
7. no cell wall			
8. animal cell			
9. plant cell			
10. cell membrane			

Analyze: Can you relate the parts of a cell to your school? Match each cell part with the corresponding school area or part.

_____ 1. Cell wall   A. Storage room

_____ 2. Vacuole   B. Doors and windows

_____ 3. Chloroplast   C. Principal's office

_____ 4. Nucleus   D. Bricks of the building

_____ 5. Cell membrane   E. Cafeteria

Name: _____   Date: _____

Creative Activities—Let's "Cell"-a-brate!

To the student observer: Choose one of the creative activities listed below to show off your creativity, while proving you understand that the cell is three-dimensional and an important part of all organisms. You must meet the criteria as stated in each of the projects. Good luck and have a great time!

Modeling: Activity One

1. Build or design a 3-D model of a cell.
2. Choose either a plant or an animal cell.
3. Include the proper organelles—choose objects that make a good representation of the organelle.
4. Create a key to identify parts.
5. Present to the class on the designated due date. Due _____

Modeling: Activity Two

1. Make a cell analogy cartoon.
2. Use any information from the cell parts lessons.
3. Make the analogy between real-world and cell part.
4. Make sure the analogy is appropriate—that it makes sense.
5. The cartoon should be drawn and colored on a single sheet of unlined paper.
6. Present the cartoon to the class and give a complete explanation on the designated due date. Due _____

Creative Writing: Activity Three

1. Write a story about a particular organelle—this will be the main character.
2. Your story should have a conflict with another organelle. The problem should be resolved by the end of the story.
3. The story must be accurate in its portrayal of the organelle.
4. Be creative—keep your reader's attention by developing your characters by using humor, etc.
5. Present your story to the class on the designated due date. Due _____

Staying Alive

Living or Nonliving

How do you tell the difference between living and nonliving things? You observe their properties. A **property** is a quality that describes an object. For example, a property of rocks (nonliving) is hardness. It is not always easy to decide if something is living or nonliving. Nonliving things can do some of the same things as living things. A robot is able to move and sometimes communicate or speak like a real person. However, a robot is not an organism. Nonliving things may carry out some of the characteristics of living things, but they will not carry out all of them.

Like nonliving things, living things have properties that you can see and feel. You have learned that cells are the basic units of life in multicellular organisms and that a single cell can carry out life activities. Most living things carry on the same kinds of activities. It is these activities that allow organisms, or living things, to stay alive. Let's take a closer look at the characteristics of life. Biologists use these main characteristics to determine if something is living or nonliving.

Characteristics of Life

- Organisms must be made up of one or more cells. The cell is the basic unit of structure and function in all-living things.
- All living things use and need energy to carry out life activities. Organisms use energy that originates from the sun. Green plants use the sun's energy to make their own food; plants make sugar from carbon dioxide and water in the presence of sunlight to carry out a process called photosynthesis. Animals get energy from the sun by eating plants or other animals that have eaten plants.
- Living things use food and excrete waste. Digestion is a life activity that breaks down food into chemicals that cells can use. Respiration is another life activity that uses oxygen to release energy that is stored in the chemicals. Respiration also produces waste. All living things excrete waste.
- Organisms must be adapted, or suited, to their surroundings. All living things have special features that help them survive in their environment.
- All living things respond to changes in their surroundings. Organisms must react to changes in their environment. You might respond to the honking of a horn by jumping and moving out of the way.
- All living things reproduce organisms like themselves. Organisms produce more organisms of their own kind. This is how life continues on Earth.
- All organisms grow and develop. Living things grow and change during their lifetime. Some, such as the frog, go through a complete change in appearance. Organisms have a life span—a beginning and an end.

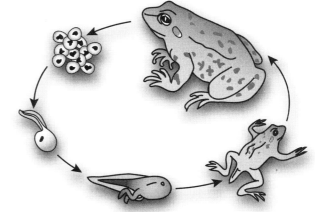

Staying Alive (cont.)

Needs of Living Things—Chemicals for Life

Food and Water

Besides being composed of cells, living things are alike because they have similar chemicals. Living things need and use these chemicals to stay alive. All organisms need food for growth and energy. Food is the fuel that provides energy to carry on various life activities. **Carbohydrates** (sugars and starches) are the fuel chemicals in your body. Carbohydrates work like gasoline in your car. Gasoline gets to the engine where it is broken down, and energy is released and runs the engine. When carbohydrates are broken down in your body, energy is released.

About two-thirds of your body is water. Humans can survive several weeks without food but only a few days without water. Water is a useful chemical. It dissolves other chemicals by breaking them down into tiny particles small enough to go in and out of the cells. When you put sugar into a glass of tea, you stir the liquid until the sugar dissolves. As it dissolves, it breaks into tiny particles you can no longer see. When the tea, sugar, and water are equally mixed, a solution is formed.

Other important chemicals found in living things are **fats**, **proteins**, and other **nutrients**. **Fats** store large amounts of energy that are released when broken down. **Proteins** are needed by the organism to build and repair body parts and regulate body activities. Proteins are basic parts of living cells. There are many different kinds of protein in your body. They help you digest food, fight infection, and keep the body running smoothly. Other **nutrients**, such as minerals and vitamins, are needed in small amounts and come from a variety of foods. To be healthy, living things need the right amount of nutrients daily.

Air

Without **air** (a mixture of gases), most living things would die in minutes. **Oxygen** is one of the gases in air. Oxygen is key in changing food into energy. Land animals get oxygen from the air they breathe. Aquatic (water) organisms get oxygen from water.

Temperature

All living things need a proper temperature to carry out life processes. Most living things could only live in a narrow temperature range if it were not for homeostasis. **Homeostasis** (hoh mee oh STAY sis) is the ability of organisms to maintain their internal conditions. Organisms need to keep conditions inside their body constant to keep things working properly.

Space

Living things need their space. They compete for enough space to get the things they need in order to survive. The living space must provide enough air, water, sunlight, food, shelter, and even mates.

Name: _____ Date: _____

Staying Alive: *Reinforcement Activity*

To the student observer: Explain what a property is and give an example.

_____

_____

_____

Analyze: In your opinion, could a butterfly be the offspring of an ant? Explain.

_____

_____

Directions: Complete the following.

1. All _____ are made up of one or more cells.

2. Organisms need and use _____ that originates from the sun.

3. Organisms respond to _____ in their surroundings.

4. Organisms must have special traits and be well _____ to their surroundings.

5. Growth and _____ are changes an organism goes through during its lifetime.

6. List five chemicals that living things need in order to stay alive.

    a. _____   b. _____

    c. _____   d. _____

               e. _____

7. Organisms need _____, a mixture of gases.

8. _____ is the ability of an organism to maintain a stable internal environment.

9. Organisms need a proper temperature and enough living _____.

10. **Predict:** What do you think would happen to an organism if its living space was destroyed? _____

    _____

The Big M—Mitosis and Meiosis

One Becomes Two—Cell Reproduction

All organisms need to grow and repair themselves by reproducing cells in a process called mitosis. Cells, like all organisms, need to grow, develop, and reproduce. In cells that have a nucleus, asexual reproduction occurs. **Asexual reproduction** is when one parent produces offspring that is an exact copy of the parent organism. In order for a cell to reproduce, it must first copy everything inside of it. Once the cell has been duplicated (copied), it then begins to split, or divide. The process of a cell dividing is called mitosis. **Mitosis** is the division of a cell's nucleus. Every living thing begins as a single cell. If cells couldn't reproduce to make complete new cells, life on Earth would cease to exist.

About Mitosis

The cell has copied its DNA, which is found in the cell's nucleus in rod-shaped struc- tures called **chromosomes**. **Deoxyribonucleic acid (DNA)** is the genetic blueprint for the organism. Your DNA carries the information for your height, eye color, and so on. A cell divides in two steps: the nucleus divides first, then the cytoplasm divides. The diagram on the next page shows the main steps in mitosis and cell division. With the DNA material copied, the cell is now ready to undergo the following steps. The nucleus disappears. The pairs (the original chromosome and the copy) line up in the center of the cell. Then the members of each pair separate and move to opposite ends of the cell. Next, the cell pinches in between the two sets of chromosomes. A nucleus forms around each set of chromosomes, forming two identical cells. Each new cell, called a **daughter cell**, has an exact copy of the chromosomes that were in the parent cell.

The Main Phases of Mitosis

Phase 1: Interphase: DNA breaks up into short chromosomes. Each chromosome makes an exact copy of itself. Each pair is attached in the middle (centromere).

Phase 2: Prophase: Chromosomes are now visible; the nuclear membrane disappears, and spindle fibers stretch across the cell. (centrioles)

Phase 3: Metaphase: Chromosomes line up along the center of the cell and attach to a spindle fiber.

Phase 4: Anaphase: Spindle fibers go to work like a tugboat, pulling each pair apart toward opposite ends of the cell.

Phase 5: Telophase: A nuclear membrane reappears around each mass of chromosomes, and the cell pinches apart in the middle. ("furrowing" in animal cells and "division plate forma- tion" in plant cells)

The Big M—Mitosis and Meiosis (cont.)

MITOSIS

1. Interphase   2. Prophase   3. Metaphase   4. Anaphase   5. Telophase

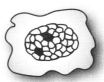    

About Meiosis

Reproduction by meiosis is a process about cutting down the numbers. All organisms have a specific number of chromosomes. You have 23 pairs of, or 46, chromosomes. Because we reproduce by sexual reproduction (two parents producing offspring), nature was faced with a particular problem. How to keep the offspring, formed by the joining of two cells, from ending up with double the number of chromosomes needed. Nature has a chromosome-reducing process in the reproductive cells (sperm cells and egg cells) called **meiosis**. The reproductive cells are called **gametes** and contain one-half the number of chromosomes found in the species' non-reproductive cells, or body cells. The human reproductive cell, or gamete, has 23 chromosomes in its nucleus. Meiosis is the cell division process that produces egg and sperm cells. When reproductive cells unite, the full number of chromosomes for the formation of body cells is restored. The reproductive cell also has traits, or genetic material, from both parents.

Meiosis requires the nucleus to divide twice—Meiosis I and Meiosis II. Meiosis I has steps and names like that of mitosis. During **Meiosis I**, the cell divides, forming two daughter cells with chromosomes still in pairs. However, in meiosis, unlike mitosis, each newly formed daughter cell divides once again. In **Meiosis II**, the chromosomes do not replicate themselves before dividing. In this way, one original cell produces four reproductive cells. Since each cell division occurs twice, each reproductive cell contains one-half the number of chromosomes as the original parent cell. Upon the union of the two reproductive cells (**fertilization**), the cell that is formed, or **zygote**, begins to develop into a new organism. The zygote has a complete set of chromosomes. One-half of the chromosomes came from the sperm cell; the other half came from the egg cell.

MEIOSIS

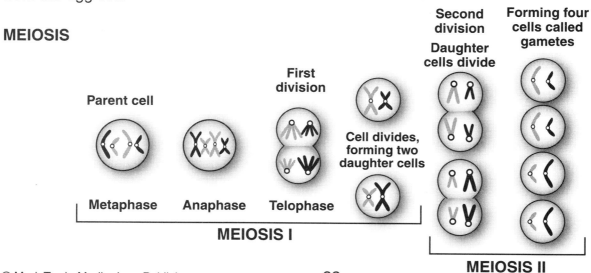

Name: _____ Date: _____

The Big M—Mitosis and Meiosis: *Reinforcement Activity*

To the student observer: Is cell division a form of reproduction? Explain. Why do you think this?

_____

_____

_____

Analyze: Why is it important that the chromosomes make exact copies of themselves before

the cell divides? _____

_____

Part I. Directions: Complete the following.

1. _____ reproduction is when one parent produces offspring

   that is an exact copy of the parent.

2. The process of cell division is called _____.

3. Your _____ carries all the information, or a blueprint, for the

   traits you have inherited from your parents.

4. The two new cells formed by mitosis are called _____ _____.

5. When a cell divides, the _____ divides first, then the

   _____ divides.

6. Reproductive cells are called _____.

7. In meiosis, the nucleus divides _____, and during mitosis, the

   nucleus divides _____.

8. Reproductive cells contain half the number of _____ of the

   body cell.

9. Humans have _____ pairs of chromosomes in all their body cells.

Part II. Directions: Match the phase of mitosis to its description.

_____ 1. Chromosomes make exact copies of themselves.

_____ 2. The nucleus disappears, and fibers stretch across the cell.

_____ 3. Chromosome pairs line up in the center of the cell.

_____ 4. Chromosome pairs are tugged to opposite ends of the cell.

_____ 5. Nuclear membranes form around each mass of
chromosomes, and the cell pinches apart, forming two daughter cells.

A. Telophase

B. Prophase

C. Anaphase

D. Interphase

E. Metaphase

33

Cells At Work—Diffusion and Osmosis

Maintaining Balance

Diffusion

The cell's membrane has a very important job. The membrane controls what enters and leaves a cell. The cell needs to maintain its required amounts of water, glucose, and other nutrients, while allowing the elimination of waste. The materials that move into and out of cells are atoms, molecules, and compounds. A **molecule** is the smallest part of a substance that is still that substance. Molecules are made up of tiny parts called **atoms**. Molecules are always moving. Molecules need their space. Molecules are constantly moving from areas where they are more crowded to areas where they are less crowded. The movement of molecules from crowded areas to less crowded areas is called **diffusion**. For example, if you bake bread in the oven, the molecules that carry the scent of baking bread will diffuse throughout the kitchen. Compounds may be organic (containing carbon), such as carbohydrates, lipids, proteins, and nucleic acids. These **organic** compounds all share one important element, carbon. **Inorganic compounds** lack the element carbon.

Diffusion in cells keeps all life processes balanced and everything working as it should. In order for a cell to carry on its life processes, oxygen and other substances must pass through the cell's membrane, and waste products must be removed from the cell. The membrane has tiny holes in it. Substances can go in and out by moving through the tiny holes. The molecules will continue to move from one area to another until the number of molecules is equal in the two areas. When this occurs, **equilibrium** is reached, and the diffusion stops. (See figure below.) After equilibrium occurs, it is maintained because molecules continue to move in order to maintain that balance.

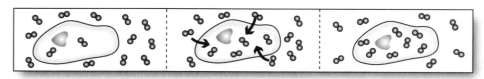

Osmosis—A Special Kind of Diffusion

One important inorganic compound living things need is water. All chemical reactions in living things take place in water solutions, and most living things use water to transport needed materials throughout their bodies. About two-thirds of your body's water is located within your body cells. Water helps to maintain the cells' shapes and sizes. The water keeps the cells' temperature constant, which allows life chemical reactions to occur. Cells contain water and are surrounded by water. Water molecules move by diffusion into and out of the cell. The diffusion of water through the cell's membrane is called **osmosis** (ahs MOH sis). Osmosis is a special kind of diffusion. Did you know that animal cells, unlike plant cells, will actually burst if too much water enters the cell?

Facilitated Diffusion

Some substances pass easily through the cell membrane by diffusion. Other substances are too large to pass through easily and can only enter the cell with the help of molecules in the cell membrane called **transport proteins**. This process, a type of passive transport, works much like the window of a drive-through restaurant. The window lets you get food out of the restaurant and put money into the restaurant.

Name: _____ Date: _____

ᴖ Diffusion and Osmosis: *Reinforcement Activity #1* ᴖ

To the student observer: Explain osmosis. _____

_____

_____

Analyze: How does osmosis explain what happens to a bowl of strawberries when you cover it with sugar? _____

_____

Part I. Directions: Complete the following.

1. Molecules are made up of small parts called _____.

2. By diffusion, molecules randomly move from _____ crowded areas to _____ crowded areas.

3. Organic compounds contain the element _____.

4. Most chemical reactions take place in _____ solutions.

5. Some substances, such as glucose, move by _____ transport with help from transport proteins in the cell's membrane.

6. When the number of molecules is equal in both areas (inside and outside the cell), _____ is reached, and diffusion stops.

Part II. Directions: Explain the way in which the molecules will move in the future to reach equilibrium (inside, outside, or equilibrium) for the cells described below.

Cell 1: _____   Cell 2: _____   Cell 3: _____

Name: _____   Date: _____

Diffusion and Osmosis: *Reinforcement Activity #2*

Observing and Measuring Osmosis

To the student observer: It is very difficult to visualize materials moving in and out of a cell and see osmosis occurring because most cells are so small. Some cells can be seen without the use of a microscope. Try this activity to see how osmosis occurs.

PROBLEM: How does osmosis occur in an egg cell?

Materials:
Unshelled egg – Use vinegar to dissolve the shell; cover raw eggs with vinegar and leave undisturbed for three days.
Balance
Slotted spoon
Distilled water (250 mL)
Corn syrup (250 mL)
500 mL container or beaker

Safety:
   Eggs may contain harmful bacteria, so wash your hands and do not touch your face while working. Unshelled eggs are very fragile—handle with care and keep them moist to avoid breaking the membranes.

Procedure:
1. Copy this table into your science journal and use it to record data.

	Beginning egg mass	Egg mass after 2 days
Distilled Water		
Corn Syrup		

2. Obtain an unshelled egg—handle carefully. Use a balance to find the egg's mass and record it in the table.
3. Place the egg in a container and add enough distilled water to cover it.
4. Observe the egg after one day and two days.
5. After day two, remove the egg with a slotted spoon and allow it to drain. Calculate the egg's mass and record it in the table. Place on a moist petri dish or towel.
6. Empty the container and put the egg back in. Now add enough corn syrup to cover the egg. Repeat steps 4 and 5.

Conclusion and Analysis:
1. **Explain** what you observed happening to the egg in the water and in the corn syrup.
2. **Calculate** the mass of water that moved into and out of the egg.
3. **Hypothesize:** Why was vinegar used for this investigation? Why was this an important step?
4. **Infer:** What part of the egg controlled the water's movement into and out of the egg?

Cells At Work—Photosynthesis and Respiration

Obtaining and Using Energy

When someone asks, "Where do you get your energy?", the simplest answer is "from the food I eat." Life is filled with many cycles. Two types of organelles, **chloroplasts** and **mitochondria**, are involved in a cycle that is necessary for the lives of plants and animals. Through the processes of photosynthesis and respiration, chemical reactions occur in cells that change the energy stored into forms needed to perform all the activities necessary for life. This allows plants and animals to get the materials they need from one another. The sum total of all your chemical reactions is called **metabolism**. All chemical reactions need enzymes. An **enzyme** is a substance that speeds up the chemical changes by the breaking down and joining of molecules. Without the right enzymes, chemical reactions in cells cannot take place. Because of **photosynthesis** (foht oh SIN thuh sis) and **respiration**, the sun's energy is used. **Photosynthesis** is the food-making process in plant cells. **Cellular respiration** is the energy-releasing process in cells. So now you are ready to put it all together to understand this sugar-making to sugar-burning process.

Photosynthesis: Sugar-Making

Photosynthesis is the reason plants do not have to eat. They use their leaves as food factories. Photosynthesis is a food-making process that uses sunlight. The food made by the plant is a sugar called **glucose**. Plants can change glucose into **nutrients** (starch, fats, and proteins) to be stored and used later.

During photosynthesis, water and carbon dioxide, in the presence of sunlight, are used to make sugar. The water and carbon dioxide are the raw materials used to produce the food, or glucose. Roots absorb the water from the soil, and veins carry the water up and into the leaves. Carbon dioxide enters the leaf through tiny openings called **stomata**. Sunlight then provides the plant with the energy needed to change the raw materials into glucose, a product the plant needs and uses. The extra molecules produce oxygen and water, which is then given off by the plant as a waste product. Simply stated, plants capture the energy in sunlight and use it to convert carbon dioxide and water into a sugar that is used for the plant's life processes. The "extra" glucose is stored in the parts of plants we eat—fruits and vegetables.

The process cannot occur without **chlorophyll** (KLOR uh fil). Chlorophyll is a green chemical pigment found in the cell's chloroplasts. Chloroplasts are mostly found in the plant's leaves, which is why the leaves are often called food factories. Photosynthesis can only occur in plant cells that contain chlorophyll. Photosynthesis releases more oxygen than the plant needs for cellular respiration, so the "extra" oxygen is released into the air. You use the oxygen to breathe for your own cellular respiration.

Respiration: Sugar-Burning

Many students believe that plants do not need oxygen. All plants respire just as we do. There are two types of respiration. One is like our method of respiration; the plant takes in the oxygen through its leaves and releases carbon dioxide. The other, cellular respiration, occurs inside the cell's mitochondria. **Cellular respiration** is the process of breaking down nutrients to create energy for cell processes. This breakdown occurs in all cells in all organs. When cells break down nutrients, wastes, such as carbon dioxide, are produced. You inhale oxygen

Cells At Work—Photosynthesis and Respiration (cont.)

and exhale carbon dioxide. Have you ever breathed on a mirror before? Did you see a fog on the glass? The fog is actually water vapor you exhaled along with the carbon dioxide. During respiration, chemical reactions (changes) occur that break down food molecules into simpler substances and release stored energy. Just as with photosynthesis, enzymes are needed for the chemical reactions to take place.

What happens when you run—do you begin to breathe faster and feel hot? Why does this happen? It's because your muscle cells use a lot of energy when you run. To get the needed energy, your muscle cells break down food. Your muscles use some of the energy created from the breakdown of your food as you move. Some of the energy becomes thermal energy, which is why you feel hot. Most cells need oxygen in order to break down the food; this is why you breathe so fast. Your muscle cells need and use the oxygen for the process of respiration. In respiration, chemical reactions occur that break down food molecules into a simpler substance and release stored energy. Review the chemical equation for photosynthesis and respiration. Then make a comparison of the two equations.

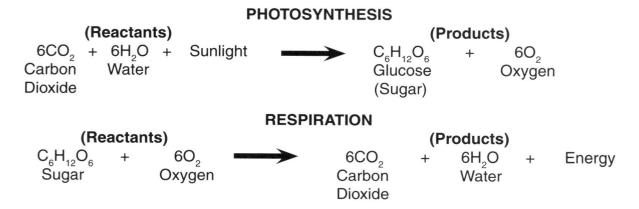

PHOTOSYNTHESIS

(Reactants)

$$6CO_2 + 6H_2O + Sunlight \longrightarrow C_6H_{12}O_6 + 6O_2$$

Carbon Dioxide Water Glucose (Sugar) Oxygen

(Products)

RESPIRATION

(Reactants)

$$C_6H_{12}O_6 + 6O_2 \longrightarrow 6CO_2 + 6H_2O + Energy$$

Sugar Oxygen Carbon Dioxide Water

(Products)

The Chemistry Behind It All

Compounds are represented by a **chemical formula**. Formulas show how many and what type of atoms are found in one molecule of the compound. The small numbers, subscripts, show how many atoms of each element it takes to make the compound. For example, there are 24 atoms in one molecule of sugar. It takes 6 carbon, 12 hydrogen, and 6 oxygen atoms to make one molecule of sugar. The large numbers in front of the compound formula, coefficients, indicate how many molecules of each compound are needed.

Sunlight and plant and cell structure for photosynthesis

Plant and animal and cell structure for respiration

38

Name: _____ Date: _____

Photosynthesis and Respiration: *Reinforcement Activity*

To the student observer: Explain why a plant does not have to eat.

_____

_____

Analyze: Compare the process of respiration to photosynthesis.

_____

_____

Part I. Directions: Complete the following.

1. The food that plants make is _____.

2. The materials a plant uses to make sugar are _____

    and _____.

3. Photosynthesis occurs in cells that contain _____.

4. A chemical formula shows the kind and number of atoms that form a_____.

5. Organic compounds contain the element _____.

6. Plants use _____ energy from the sun to make glucose.

7. Metabolism is the total of all _____ _____ in an organism.

8. _____ occurs in the mitochondria in all cells.

9. _____ speed up chemical changes.

10. Chemical reactions take place in _____ solutions.

Part II. Directions: Write "P" if it describes photosynthesis or "R" if it describes respiration.

_____ 1. Carbon dioxide is waste.

_____ 2. Occurs in the chloroplasts of plant cells

_____ 3. Oxygen is given off.

_____ 4. Energy is stored.

_____ 5. Energy is burned or released.

_____ 6. Occurs in the mitochondria of all cells

Name: _____ Date: _____

Cell Vocabulary: *Study Sheet*

1. **Cell** - the basic unit of life

2. **Cell membrane** - a thin structure that surrounds the cell and controls the movement of materials into and out of the cell

3. **Cell wall** - the outer, nonliving part of a plant cell that provides structure to the cell

4. **Chloroplast** - a green disc-shaped organelle in plants that captures sunlight for making food

5. **Cytoplasm** - a gel-like substance inside a cell that contains all of the living material except the nucleus

6. **Deoxyribonucleic acid (DNA)** - the chemical contained in chromosomes that stores information about an organism

7. **Diffusion** - the movement of material from an area where molecules are crowded to an area where they are less crowded

8. **Electron microscope** - instruments that use beams of electrons to magnify things

9. **Endoplasmic reticulum (ER)** - a system of tubes that processes and moves proteins within the cell

10. **Golgi bodies** - package and distribute proteins outside the cell.

11. **Homeostasis** - the ability of organisms to maintain a constant internal condition

12. **Lysosome** - a tiny organelle that breaks down substances (digests waste)

13. **Meiosis** - the process of cell division that results in reproductive cells

14. **Mitochondria** - organelles that use oxygen to release energy for the cell (power supply)

15. **Mitosis** - the process of cell division that results in two cells identical to the parent cell

16. **Nucleus** - the structure in the cell that controls all cell activities

17. **Organ** - a group of different tissues that work together to do a certain job

18. **Organelle** - a small structure inside a cell that performs a certain job

19. **Organism** - a living thing

20. **Osmosis** - the diffusion of water through a cell membrane

21. **Ribosome** - a small, round structure that makes proteins

22. **Tissue** - a group of cells that look alike and work together to do a certain job

23. **Vacuole** - a liquid-filled structure in a cell that stores food, water, and waste

Name: _____ Date: _____

Cell Unit Test

Part I. Directions: Put the correct answer on the blank.

_____ 1. A microscope containing two or more lenses is a(n) _____ microscope.
   a. compound   b. electron   c. simple   d. stereoscope

_____ 2. Genes on chromosomes inside the cell _____ control inherited traits.
   a. cytoplasm   b. mitochondria   c. Golgi bodies   d. nucleus

_____ 3. All living things are made up of
   a. only one cell.   b. one or more cells.   c. many cells.   d. tissues.

_____ 4. Reproduction, digestion, movement, and growth are examples of
   a. homeostasis.   b. development.   c. life activities.   d. mitosis.

_____ 5. A cell is often defined as a basic unit of _____ in all living things.
   a. protein   b. structure   c. reproduction   d. nutrition

_____ 6. The simplest cells in existence are _____ cells.
   a. bacteria   b. protist   c. fungi   d. plant

_____ 7. _____ in your body send and receive messages.
   a. Blood cells   b. Immune cells   c. Nerve cells   d. Bone cells

_____ 8. Similar cells that work together make up
   a. organs.   b. tissue.   c. organisms.   d. systems.

_____ 9. An English scientist, _____ _____, was the first person to view cells.
   a. Anton van Leeuwenhoek   b. Randolph Virchow
   c. Robert Hooke   d. Alexander Fleming

_____ 10. To calculate the magnification of a microscope, you _____ the magnification of the eyepiece lens and that of the objective lens.
   a. add   b. subtract   c. divide   d. multiply

_____ 11. A(n) _____ microscope has the greatest magnification and is used to study cells.
   a. complex   b. compound   c. electron   d. stereoscope

Name: _____ Date: _____

Cell Unit Test (cont.)

_____ 12. _____ are small structures that float in the gel-like cytoplasm.
a. Vacuoles   b. Chloroplasts   c. Organelles   d. Organisms

_____ 13. Most cells, except bacteria, are
a. eukaryotic.   b. prokaryotic.   c. atypical.   d. typical.

_____ 14. The three main parts of a cell are the nucleus, the cell membrane, and the
a. plasma.   b. ribosome.   c. cytoplasm.   d. chromosome.

_____ 15. Most of the cells in your body reproduce by a process called
a. mitosis.   b. meiosis.   c. osmosis.   d. diffusion.

_____ 16. Humans have _____ chromosomes.
a. 23   b. 23 pairs of   c. 46 pairs of   d. 64

_____ 17. In mitosis, the two newly formed cells are called
a. son cells.   b. twin cells.   c. daughter cells.   d. mitosis cells.

_____ 18. Substances must move in and out of the cell by a process called
a. osmosis.   b. diffusion.   c. respiration.   d. photosynthesis.

_____ 19. _____ is the movement of water through the cell's membrane.
a. Osmosis   b. Diffusion   c. Respiration   d. Photosynthesis

_____ 20. Particles continue to move from being crowded to being less crowded until _____ is reached.
a. homeostasis   b. equilibrium   c. cytosis   d. photosynthesis

_____ 21. A group of tissues that work together make up a(n)
a. cell.   b. organ.   c. system.   d. organism.

_____ 22. During _____, the sun's energy is trapped in plant cells.
a. photosynthesis   b. respiration   c. homeostasis   d. equilibrium

_____ 23. During _____, food is broken down, and energy is released.
a. photosynthesis   b. respiration   c. homeostasis   d. equilibrium

Name: _____ Date: _____

Cell Unit Test (cont.)

Part II. Directions. Match each of the following descriptions below.

_____ 24. Controls the cell's activities

_____ 25. The powerhouse of the cell

_____ 26. Transportation network

_____ 27. Gel-like material inside the cell

_____ 28. Building blocks of life

_____ 29. Reproductive cells

_____ 30. Food-making structure in a plant cell

_____ 31. Stores water, food, and waste

_____ 32. Surrounds the cell membrane in plant cells

_____ 33. Makes protein for the cell

_____ 34. Shapes and protects the cell

_____ 35. Inside the nucleus; contains DNA

a. Vacuole

b. Ribosomes

c. Cell wall

d. Endoplasmic reticulum (ER)

e. Mitochondrion

f. Nucleus

g. Chloroplast

h. Cytoplasm

i. Cells

j. Gametes

k. Chromosomes

l. Cell membrane

Part III. Directions: Write "A" above the animal cell and "P" above the plant cell and identify the structures.

1. _____

2. _____

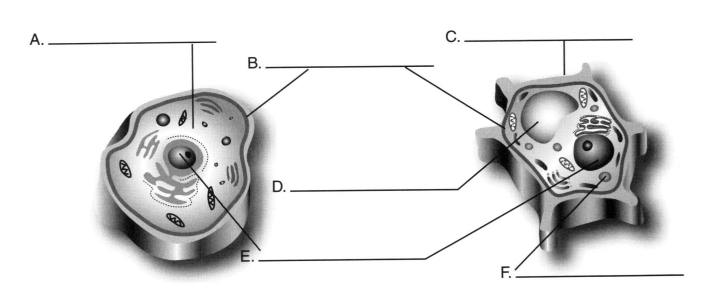

A. _____

B. _____

C. _____

D. _____

E. _____

F. _____

Answer Keys

What Are Cells?: Reinforcement Activity (p. 4)
To the student observer: Any logical answer; teacher check.
Analyze: As microscopes improved, we learned more about cells.
Part I
1. Cells
2. specialized
3. found
4. many
5. one
6. simplest

Part II
1. C   2. D   3. F   4. E   5. B   6. A

Part III
a. Bacteria or Monera
b. Protista
c. Fungi
d. Plants
e. Animals

Let's Get Organized!: Reinforcement Activity (p. 7)
To the student observer: Any logical answer; teacher check.
Analyze:
Organelles ⟶ Cells ⟶ Tissue ⟶
Organs ⟶ Systems ⟶ Organisms
Molecule is not used. I organized them from smallest to largest. **Students may reverse the order, working from largest to smallest.
1. Organelles
2. Cells
3. tissue
4. organ
5. system

6a. Skeletal system
b. Muscular system
c. Digestive system
d. Circulatory system
e. Respiratory system
f. Excretory system
g. Nervous system

7a. Muscle tissue
b. Covering tissue
c. Connective tissue
d. Nerve tissue

The History of Cells: Reinforcement Activity (p. 10)
To the student observer: Any of these: Anton van Leeuwenhoek, Theodor Schwann, Matthias Schleiden
Analyze: No, the cork was no longer living. Only living cells can make new cells.
1. Cells
2. Robert Hooke
3. cork
4. Anton van Leeuwenhoek
5. Cell Theory
6. Schleiden, Schwann, Virchow
7. Histologists
8a. All organisms are made up of one or many cells.
b. Cells are the basic units of structure and function in all organisms.
c. All cells come from other cells that already exist.

What Is a Microscope?: Reinforcement Activity (p. 14)
To the student observer: To look at very small things; *micro* means "very small," and *scope* means "to look at."
Analyze: You see less of the object in your field of view, but you see greater detail. It zooms in the image.
1. It has two or more lenses.
2. 550X; multiply 10 x 55 = 550
3. Compound light microscope
4. A convex lens curves outward.
5. An electron microscope
6. A stereoscope microscope

The Parts of a Microscope (p. 16)
A. **Eyepiece** – contains the lens you look through; the top part of the microscope.
B. **Body tube** - Light passes through this hollow tube; it also maintains the correct distance between the eyepiece lens and the objective lens.
C. **Nosepiece** – (revolving) holds the objective lenses and rotates to change the magnification.
D. **Objective lenses** – usually from 10X to 40X magnification; located on the nosepiece.
E. **Stage** – supports the object (microscope slide) being viewed.
F. **Stage clips** – hold the microscope slide in place.
G. **Diaphragm** – changes the amount of light that enters the body tube
H. **Mirror or light source** – is used to send light up through the hole in the stage, the object, and the lenses.
I. **Coarse adjustment knob** - turns to raise and lower the body tube or stage for focusing; always use this knob first.
J. **Fine adjustment knob** – moves slightly and is used to sharpen the image.
K. **Arm** - supports the body tube and is used to carry the microscope.
L. **Base** - supports the microscope and is used to carry it; the bottom part of the microscope.

Microscope Quiz (p. 17)
1. C   2. L   3. G   4. A   5. F
6. B   7. I   8. J   9. E   10. D
11. M   12. H   13. K

The Parts of a Cell: Reinforcement Activity (p. 22–23)

To the student observer: Organelles are small structures inside the cytoplasm that keep the cell working or cell parts that have a special job to do.

Analyze: Muscle cells - cells need energy and muscles do a lot of work and need a lot of energy. The mitochondria are the power supply of the cell.

1. To carry out life activities or functions
2a. Nucleus - controls the cell's activities
   b. Cytoplasm - gel-like material that contains a variety of cell materials; contains the chemicals needed
   c. Cell membrane - surrounds the cell; controls the movement of materials into and out of the cell; shapes and protects the cell.
3. Ribosomes
4. Endoplasmic reticulum (ER)
5. Water, food, and waste
6 Any three: Shape; Plants have chloroplasts; Plants have cell walls; Vacuoles are larger in plant cells; Plant cells lack lysosomes
7. Cytoplasm
8. To enclose the nucleus and control movement into and out of the nucleus; shapes and protects the nucleus
9. Teacher check.

Living Things Are Made of These?: Lab Report (p. 24–26)

Viewing Cells Lab: onion, elodea, cheek cells - accept all logical drawings.

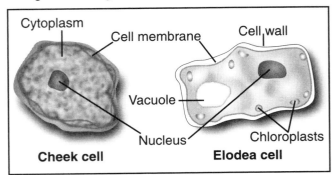

Cytoplasm | Cell membrane | Cell wall
Vacuole
Nucleus | Chloroplasts
Cheek cell | **Elodea cell**

Lab Report

Problem: Yes, plants and animals are made up of many cells. Using a microscope, these cells can be observed.

To the student observer:

1. Onion, Elodea
2. Elodea
3. All three
4. Cheek
5. Onion, Elodea
6. All three
7. Cheek
8. Cheek
9. Onion, Elodea
10. All three

Analyze:

1. D   2. A   3. E   4. C   5. B

Staying Alive: Reinforcement Activity (p. 30)

To the student observer: A property is a quality that describes an object. Hardness is an example of a property. Accept all logical answers.

Analyze: No, organisms can only make organisms like themselves.

1. organisms
2. energy
3. changes
4. adapted
5. development
6a. Water
   b. Fats
   c. Nutrients
   d. Proteins
   e. Carbohydrates
7. air
8. Homeostasis
9. space
10. It might die because it wouldn't have enough food, water, or shelter to support itself.

The Big M: Reinforcement Activity (p. 33)

To the student observer: Yes, asexual reproduction; a new cell is formed just like the parent. (It has reproduced a copy of itself.) Accept all logical answers.

Analyze: To make sure the genetic code is passed on to the new cell.

Part I

1. Asexual
2. mitosis
3. DNA
4. daughter cells
5. nucleus, cytoplasm
6. gametes
7. twice, once
8. chromosomes
9. 23

Part II

1. D   2. B   3. E   4. C   5. A

Diffusion and Osmosis: Reinforcement Activity #1 (p. 35)

To the student observer: It is the movement of water through a cell's membrane.

Analyze: To maintain equilibrium, water molecules diffuse out through the strawberries' cell membrane to where there is less water. (Molecules move from more crowded areas to less crowded areas.)

Part I

1. atoms
2. more, less
3. carbon
4. water
5. passive
6. equilibrium

Part II

Cell 1 - Inside
Cell 2 - Equilibrium
Cell 3 - Outside

Diffusion and Osmosis: Reinforcement Activity #2 (p. 36)

Teacher check.

Photosynthesis and Respiration: Reinforcement Activity (p. 39)

To the student observer: A plant can make its own food by a process called photosynthesis.

Analyze: Respiration is the opposite of photosynthesis. The reactants of the process of respiration are the products of photosynthesis.

Part I
1. glucose or sugar
2. carbon dioxide, water
3. chloroplasts or chlorophyll
4. compound
5. carbon
6. light
7. chemical reactions
8. Respiration
9. Enzymes
10. water

Part II
1. R   2. P   3. P   4. P   5. R   6. R

Cell Unit Test (p. 41–43)

Part I
1. a   2. d   3. b   4. c
5. b   6. a   7. c   8. b
9. c   10. d   11. c   12. c
13. a   14. c   15. a   16. b
17. c   18. b   19. a   20. b
21. b   22. a   23. b

Part II
24. f   25. e   26. d   27. h
28. i   29. j   30. g   31. a
32. c   33. b   34. l   35. k

Part III
1. A   2. P
A. Cytoplasm   B. Cell membrane
C. Cell wall   D. Vacuole
E. Nucleus   F. Chloroplast

Bibliography

Bernstein, Schachter, Winkler, Wolfe. *Concepts and Challenges in Life Science.* Globe, 1998.

Briggs, Daniel, and Ortleb. *Life Science.* Glencoe/McGraw-Hill, 1997.

LaRue, Charles J. *Biology.* AGS Publishing, 2004.

Pfeiffer. *The Cell.* Time-Life Books, 1972.

Young. *Cells: Amazing Forms and Functions.* Watts, 1990.